*Titles in this series:*
The Crazy World of Aerobics
The Crazy World of Cats
The Crazy World of Football
The Crazy World of Gardening
The Crazy World of Golf
The Crazy World of Hospitals
The Crazy World of Marriage
The Crazy World of The Office
The Crazy World of Photography
The Crazy World of Sailing
The Crazy World of Schools
The Crazy World of Sex

This paperback edition published simultaneously in 1992 by Exley
Publications Ltd. in Great Britain, and Exley Giftbooks in the USA.
First hardback edition published in Great Britain in 1988 by Exley
Publications Ltd.

12  11  10  9  8  7  6  5  4

Copyright © Bill Stott, 1990

ISBN 1-85015-495-3

Printed in Malta.

Exley Publications Ltd, 16 Chalk Hill, Watford, Herts WD1 4BN,
United Kingdom.
Exley Giftbooks, 232 Madison Avenue, Suite 1206, NY 10016, USA.

# THE Crazy WORLD OF FOOTBALL

## CARTOONS BY
## BILL STOTT

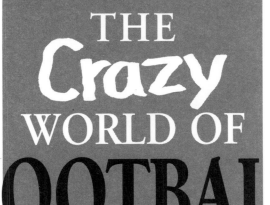

 EXLEY

NEW YORK • WATFORD, UK

*"Eh love! Before you do all the posh songs – sing one for me –
it goes...'Come on you Reds, come on you Reds' –
just the first verse will do..."*

*"I can't even <u>pronounce</u> your team, but they didn't half play well!"*

*"Hey! There's our team's banner – looks like the guys made it!"*

"...old world cheerleaders!"

"How was the match, honey?"

*"Terrible. Germany won ten nil. No crowd trouble. No sending-offs. No nothing!"*

*"Like it? That's one of the first soccer chants I ever wrote."*

"*A spectator threw a missile? You mean we've got spectators out there?*"

*"It's going to be one of those afternoons."*

*"Nobody bends a ball like Gary..."*

*"Offside, Kevin..."*

①

②

③

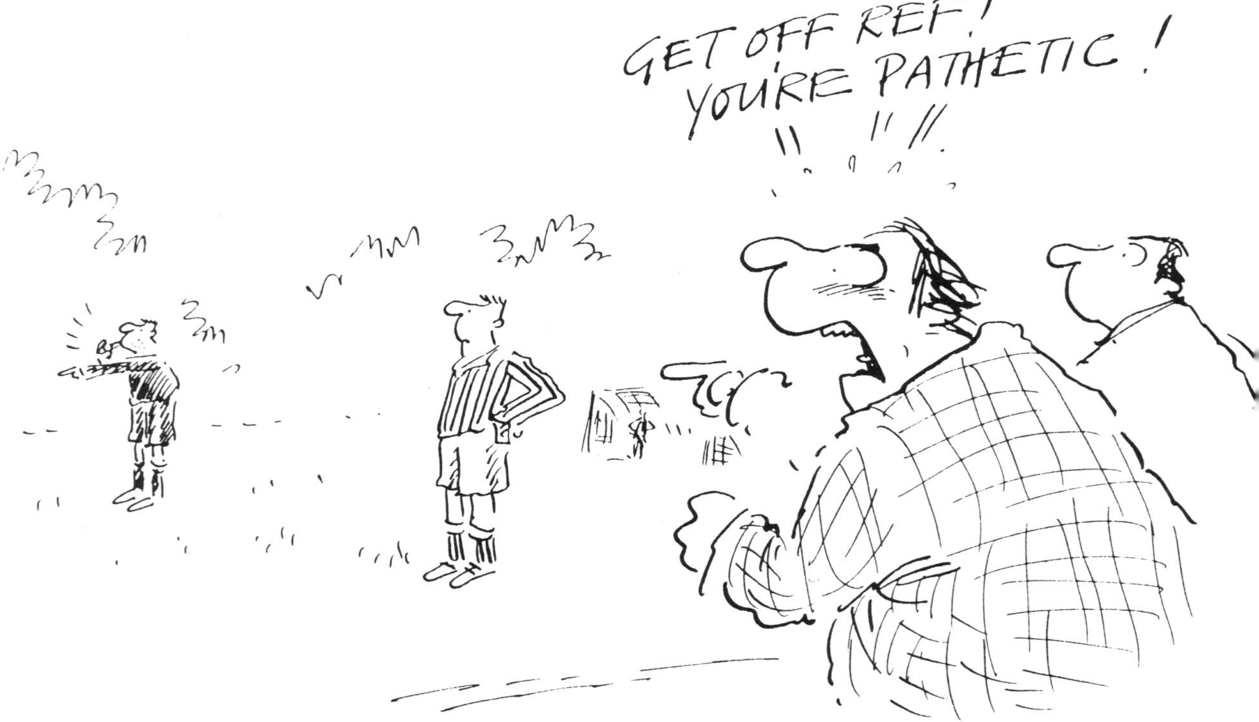
GET OFF REF! YOU'RE PATHETIC!

I BEG YOUR PARDON?

"First – my mother and father are married. Second – you were definitely offside. Third – any more language like that and I'll smack your legs!"

②

"Isn't that Saturday's ref?"

*"Huh – seven nil. We don't support our team. We prop them up!"*

*"Now! Inside! Inside! Lay it back! Go inside! No! Not that way!..."*

*...Sometimes I might as well talk to myself!"*

*"They're bound to do that – the only other time they line up together is to face a free kick..."*

①

*"Great goal, Gary. Gary?...Where's Gary?"*

*"It's that new signing Boss – the guys are just making sure he knows how to roll about and scream in agony at the slightest contact with an opposing player..."*

"There's a guy in the dugout wants a word with you.
He's a Hollywood talent scout..."

"We can't have your number six's mother rushing on every time he's brought down..."

"He's preparing for this afternoon's match."

*"I don't suppose there's anything in the rules about that, Ref?"*

"*I told you St. Dominic's were a hard lot – that's their mascot.*"

*"It's Terry's one hundredth sending-off!"*

*"Offside? Offside? The guy is blind – he is BLIND!!"*

②

*"Pardon?"*

③

*"Er, I was just saying what a brave decision that was...."*

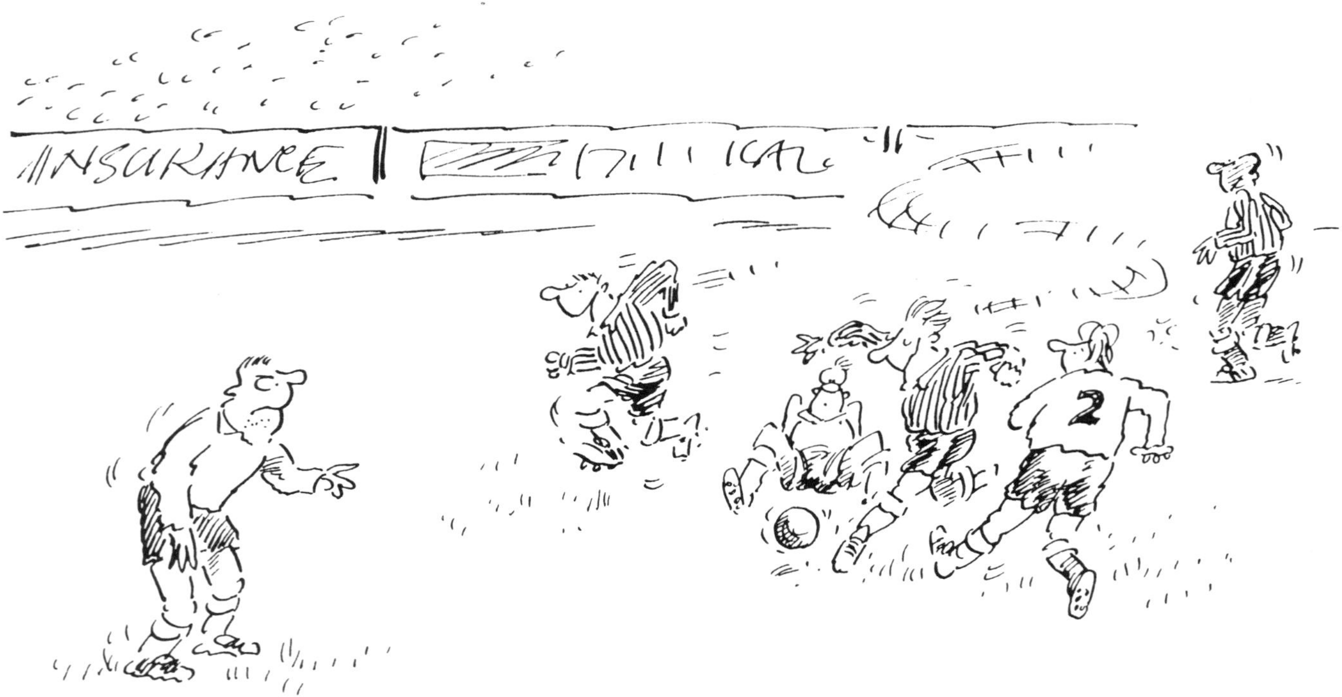
INSURANCE
2

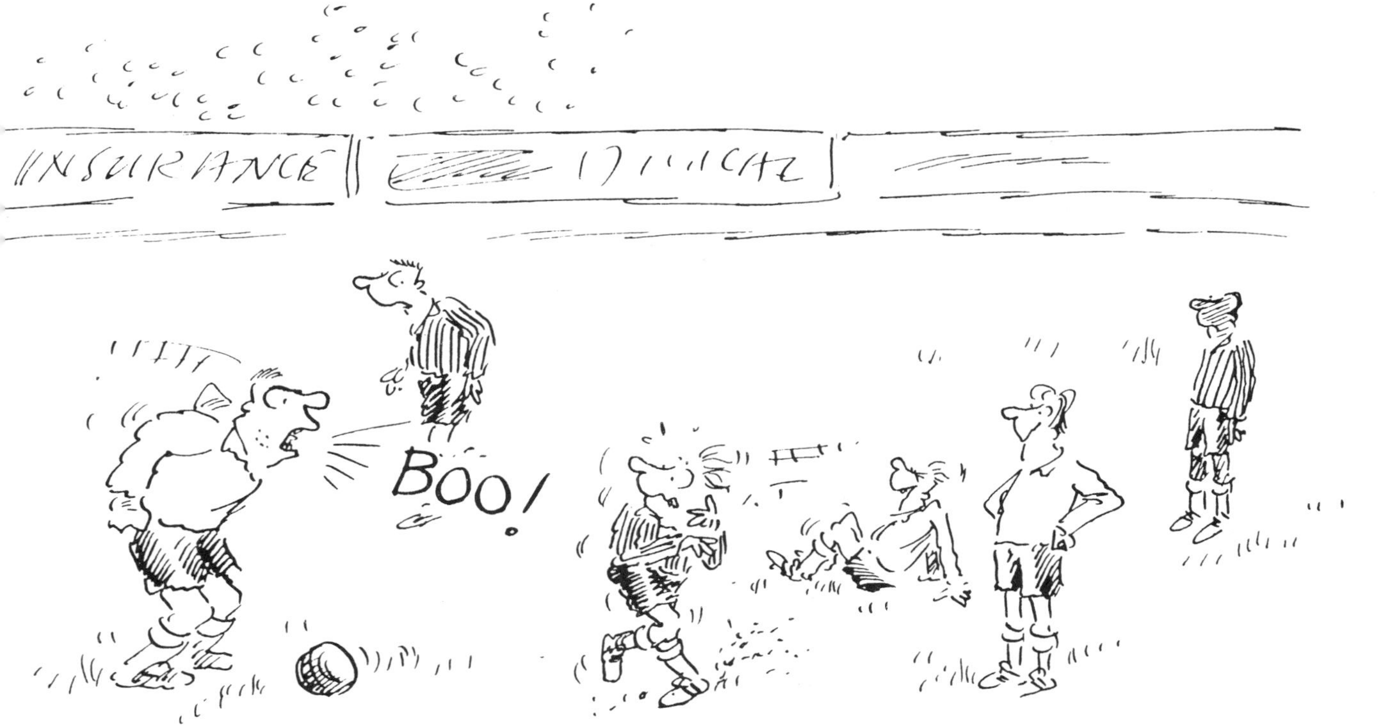
INSURANCE
BOO!

*"Smile...!"*

*"Their No. 7 was good, wasn't he?"*

*"And from here I can see that Rover's No. 7 isn't happy with that decision..."*

"*Well Brian, at the end of the day, the ref's decision is final, despite him being a two-faced, lying rat who's probably on the take.*"

"Well, we've had a pretty lively debate here tonight..."

"O.K. I want a nice open pattern – Dean and Gary making runs down the flanks, Tommo and Wayne drawing in their defenders. While all this is going on, you Eric, will run about kicking anybody you don't recognize..."

"*The boss is keeping it simple this week...*"

*"Look! A sponsor's a sponsor – now put it on!"*

*"He's going through his after-goal crowd adulation response..."*

*"Er – what I said about women physios – it was a joke – right?"*

"I don't trust that new left back – keeping his underpants
on in the shower!"

"*Your million dollar bargain just tied his own bootlaces together.*"

"Why are we out of the Cup? Well, I think it's because our team's useless and we've scored once in nineteen matches..."

*"A free transfer – good grief, no! We're paying you to go!"*

"*Your dad's applying for the manager's job. The main thrust of his argument being that he couldn't do any worse and he'd do it for half the money...*"

*"He was showing the kids some advanced tackling techniques..."*

*"Look. Just because your grandpa bought the ball doesn't mean he gets to play!"*

"*Dad says it's got no atmosphere if you watch it indoors ...*"

"Huh! They've even got better _names_ than us!"

*"After our team was knocked out – that was it – no more soccer – look at him – glued to Belgium v Mexico!"*

*"Guatemala v Equador...Oh goody!"*

*"I said, 'My mother's coming to stay for a month. The kids have run away to join the Moonies and your car's on fire!'"*

"*Do you think that if I took up soccer, your dad would do that to me?*"

"His dad's very worried about him – he wants a referee's outfit for Christmas!"

*"Then Grandad said 'Here's one I bet they don't teach you at school'
and kicked it straight through the French window..."*

"*Our Gary's soccer crazy – he's out in the yard trying out his dives...*"

*"See! I told you he could write!"*

*"Youth Club is organizing a 'Dads' and Lads''*
*match.   I was wondering if you'd care to...*

*...be a linesman?"*

*"I'm especially proud of that one – goalie's teeth, semi final, 1953..."*

**Books in "The World's Greatest" series**
($4.99  £2.50 paperback)

The World's Greatest Business Cartoons
The World's Greatest Cat Cartoons
The World's Greatest Computer Cartoons
The World's Greatest Dad Cartoons
The World's Greatest Do-It-Yourself Cartoons
The World's Greatest Golf Cartoons
The World's Greatest Keep Fit Cartoons
The World's Greatest Marriage Cartoons
The World's Greatest Middle Age Cartoons
The World's Greatest Rugby Cartoons
The World's Greatest Sex Cartoons

**Books in the "Victim's Guide" series**
($4.99  £2.50 paperback)

Award-winning cartoonist Roland Fiddy sees the funny side to life's phobias, nightmares and catastrophes.

The Victim's Guide to Air Travel
The Victim's Guide to The Baby
The Victim's Guide to The Boss
The Victim's Guide to Christmas
The Victim's Guide to The Dentist
The Victim's Guide to The Doctor
The Victim's Guide to Middle Age

**Books in the "Crazy World" series**
($4.99  £2.50 paperback)

The Crazy World of Aerobics
The Crazy World of Hospitals
The Crazy World of The Office
The Crazy World of Sailing
The Crazy World of School

The following titles in this series are available in paperback and also in a full colour mini hardback edition ($6.99 £3.99)

The Crazy World of Bowls
The Crazy World of Cats
The Crazy World of Football
The Crazy World of Gardening
The Crazy World of Golf
The Crazy World of Housework
The Crazy World of Marriage
The Crazy World of Rugby
The Crazy World of Sex

**Books in the "Fanatic's Guide" series**
($4.99  £2.50 paperback)

The **Fanatic's Guides** are perfect presents for everyone with a hobby that has got out of hand. Eighty pages of hilarious black and white cartoons by Roland Fiddy.

The Fanatic's Guide to Dogs
The Fanatic's Guide to Money
The Fanatic's Guide to Sports

The following titles in this series are available in paperback and also in a full colour mini hardback edition ($6.99 £3.99)

The Fanatic's Guide to Cats
The Fanatic's Guide to Computers
The Fanatic's Guide to Dads
The Fanatic's Guide to D.I.Y.
The Fanatic's Guide to Golf
The Fanatic's Guide to Husbands
The Fanatic's Guide to Love
The Fanatic's Guide to Sex